YORK NOTES

OF MICE AND MEN

JOHN STEINBECK

WORKBOOK BY MIKE GOULD

PEARSON

YORK PRESS

The right of Mike Gould to be identified as the Author of this Work has been asserted by him in accordance with the Copyright, Designs and Patents Act 1988

YORK PRESS
322 Old Brompton Road, London SW5 9JH

PEARSON EDUCATION LIMITED
Edinburgh Gate, Harlow,
Essex CM20 2JE, United Kingdom
Associated companies, branches and representatives throughout the world

First published 2014

10 9 8 7 6 5 4 3

ISBN 978–1–4479–8046–9

Illustrations by Bob Moulder; and Neil Gower (page 6 only)

Photo credits:
JIANG HONGYAN/Shutterstock.com for page 8 / Phent/Shutterstock.com for page 16 / Christian Weber/Shutterstock.com for page 19 / Hintau Aliaksei/Shutterstock.com for page 33

Typeset by Carnegie Book Production
Printed in Slovakia

CONTENTS

PART FOUR:
KEY CONTEXTS AND THEMES

PART FIVE:
LANGUAGE AND STRUCTURE

PART SIX:
GRADE BOOSTER

PART ONE: Introduction

How to use this workbook

WHAT IS THE WORKBOOK FOR?

This workbook is for your use during your study or revision of *Of Mice and Men*. It can be used on its own, or alongside the York Notes for GCSE: *Of Mice and Men* study guide, which is available in bookshops or online at www.yorknotes.com. It will help you:

- **Revise** the basic content of the novel – who did what? When? Where? Why?
- **Practise** key reading and writing skills, such as writing more fluent paragraphs
- **Assess** your own level by seeing other students' work and comments from experts on it

WHY A WORKBOOK?

By providing 'Progress logs', and space to write in your answers for many of the tasks, the workbook gives you a visual indication of how well you are doing. You could even share it with your English teacher if you want!

HOW IS THE WORKBOOK ORGANISED?

The workbook is divided into six main Parts and follows the same basic structure as the York Notes study guide if you want to cross-refer between them. You can:

- Follow the parts one by one, checking your knowledge and skills in stages

Or

- Dip in, selecting areas you feel most, or least, confident about

WHAT ARE THE KEY FEATURES?

There are **'Quick tests'** designed to check your knowledge through short, quick tasks such as multiple choice or 'true/false' questions.

'Thinking more deeply' requires you to write more fully (often a sentence or two) about a particular issue or character.

'Exam preparation' goes a bit further and requires you to deal with full-length questions, and plan and draft part of an exam-style answer with support to help you.

A **'Progress log'** at regular intervals allows you to keep a running record of how you are doing.

At the end of each section there is a **'Practice task'**, which gives you an even more challenging task to complete in full, as revision for your exam.

'Answers' for most tasks are supplied at the end of the workbook, but try not to look at them while you're completing the tasks, however much you are tempted! Wait until you have had one or even two attempts before you check.

Most importantly, enjoy using this workbook, and seeing your knowledge and skills improve!

The text used in this workbook is the Longman Schools Edition 2003.

Introducing *Of Mice and Men*

Before you begin this workbook, check how well you know *Of Mice and Men*.

SETTING

1 Look at the map and the diagram of the ranch below. On the map/diagram write the names of characters and events linked to each location. For example, for 'Weed' you could write 'where Lennie touched the girl's dress'.

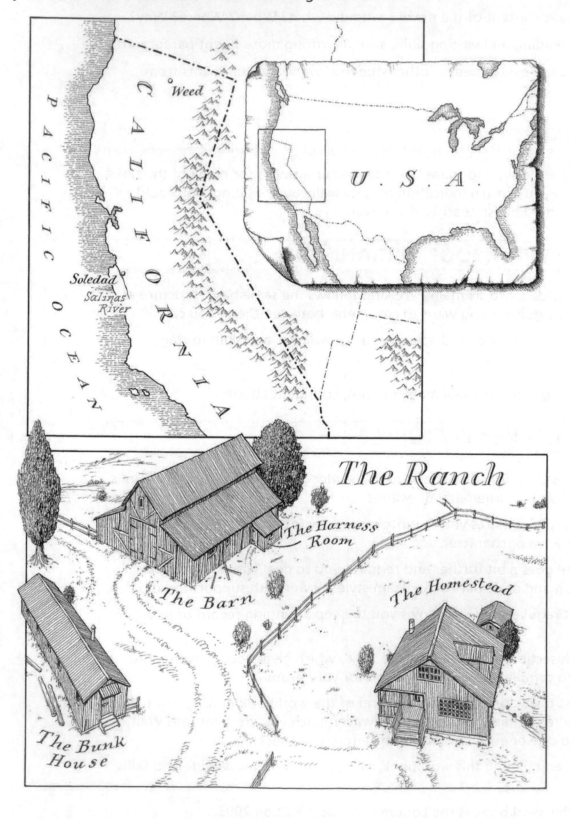

CHARACTERS: WHO'S WHO

❷ Now look at this drawing of the different characters. Without checking the novel or the York Notes study guide, write in:

The **NAME** (if known) of each person

Their **JOB** or **ROLE** at the ranch

Name: ....

Job/role: ....

Name: ....

Job/role: ....

Names: ....

....

Jobs/roles: ....

....

Name: ....

Job/role: ....

Names: ....

Jobs/roles: ....

Names: ....

Jobs/roles: ....

Name: ....

Job/role: ....

JOHN STEINBECK: AUTHOR AND CONTEXT

❸ What do you know about John Steinbeck? Circle the correct information in each line:

a) Born 27 February 1902 in <u>Salinas / Sacramento / San Diego</u>, California.

b) In 1925 suddenly leaves his <u>job / university / wife</u> and goes to New York.

c) In 1929 the 'Great <u>Fall / Crash / Flop</u>' on Wall Street starts the Great Depression.

d) In the same year, Steinbeck publishes his first <u>poem / play / novel</u>, *Cup of Gold*.

e) *Of Mice and Men* is published in <u>1934 / 1935 / 1937</u>.

f) In 1939 the <u>First / Second / Third</u> World War breaks out, not ending until 1945.

g) During the war, Steinbeck's first marriage breaks up. But his novel *The Grapes of Wrath* wins the <u>Booker / Pulitzer / Orange</u> prize.

h) In 1962, he is awarded the Nobel Prize in <u>Science / Peace / Literature</u>.

i) He dies in 1968 but is still remembered for his works, including other novels such as <u>*East of Eden / West of Eden / East of California*</u>.

PART TWO: Plot and Action

Section One: Moving on

QUICK TEST ✔

❶ Tick the box for the **correct** answer to each of these questions:

a) What has Lennie been carrying in secret?

a puppy ☐   a dead mouse ☐   a furry rabbit ☐

b) Why did George and Lennie have to leave Weed?

there was no work ☐   Lennie touched a girl's dress ☐   the weather was bad ☐

c) Where are they going?

to Aunt Clara's ☐   to a ranch for work ☐   to Soledad ☐

d) What do they plan to do when they have enough money?

go back to Weed ☐   buy a small farm and keep rabbits ☐   live in the mountains ☐

e) What does George make Lennie promise to do if there is any trouble?

return to the same pool ☐   head for the hills ☐   speak to the ranch boss ☐

THINKING MORE DEEPLY ❓

❷ Write **one** or **two sentences** in response to each of these questions:

a) In what ways do George and Lennie differ in their appearance?

....

....

....

b) What two animals does Steinbeck compare Lennie with in this scene?

....

....

....

c) Why are rabbits mentioned at the start of the novel?

....

....

....

EXAM PREPARATION: Writing about George and Lennie

Re-read the section from *'The small man stepped nervously beside him ...'* (p. 3) to *'He pulled his hat down a little more over his eyes, the way George's hat was.'* (p. 4)

Question: How do the details in this passage help you to understand the relationship between George and Lennie?

Think about:

- What they say and do in this extract

❸ Complete this table:

Point/detail	Evidence	Effect or explanation
1: George looks out for Lennie and tells him what (or what not) to do.	He uses commands such as: '... don't drink so much.'	George behaves like a parent might to a small child who can't be trusted to make his own decisions.
2: Lennie behaves and speaks in a child-like way.		
3: Lennie seeks George's approval.		

❹ Write up **point 1** into a **paragraph** below in your own words:

....

....

....

....

....

....

❺ Now, choose **one** of your **other points** and write it out as another **paragraph** here:

....

....

....

....

....

....

PROGRESS LOG [tick the correct box]   Needs more work ☐   Getting there ☐   Under control ☐

Section Two: Rising tensions

QUICK TEST

❶ **Number** the events of this section so that they are in the **correct sequence**. Use **'1'** for the first event and **'7'** for the final event:

a) The boss questions George and Lennie and gives them their job instructions.	
b) The 'old swamper' (p. 20) (Candy) shows George and Lennie into the bunk house.	
c) Candy tells George about the boss, and the 'stable buck' (p. 21) (Crooks).	
d) Slim and Carlson are introduced, before they both leave for dinner.	
e) Curley enters the bunk house and tries to pick a fight with Lennie.	
f) Curley returns to the bunk house asking if anyone has seen his wife.	
g) Curley's wife comes into the bunk house and flirts with the men.	

THINKING MORE DEEPLY

❷ Write **one** or **two sentences** in response to each of these questions:

a) Why does the boss question Lennie and George so closely?

....

....

....

b) What impression do you get of Curley from his two appearances in the bunk house?

....

....

....

c) In what way does this section 'plant the seeds' of some of the troubles that happen later in the novel?

....

....

....

....

....

EXAM PREPARATION: WRITING ABOUT THE BUNK HOUSE

Re-read the section from *'The bunk house was a long, rectangular building.'* (p. 19) to *'We don't want no pants rabbits.'* (p. 20)

Question: How do the details in this passage help you to understand the sort of life led by the men on the ranch?

Think about:

● The description of the building itself and its furniture

● The men's possessions

❸ Complete this table:

Point/detail	Evidence	Effect or explanation
1: *The minimum effort has been made to make the place liveable.*	*'… the walls were whitewashed and the floor unpainted.'*	*The bunk house is very basic and functional, and reminds everyone that this is a place of work, rather than their own home.*
2: *There is little privacy for the men.*		
3: *Space for personal possessions does exist but it is very limited.*		

❹ Write up **point 1** into a **paragraph** below in your own words:

....

....

....

....

....

❺ Now, choose **one** of your **other points** and write it out as another **paragraph** here:

....

....

....

....

....

....

PROGRESS LOG [tick the correct box]   Needs more work ☐   Getting there ☐   Under control ☐

Section Three: The dawn of hope

QUICK TEST ✓

❶ **Tick** the box for the **correct** answer to each of these questions:

a) Where were George and Lennie both born?

Soledad ☐   Auburn ☐   Sacramento ☐

b) Why does Carlson tell Candy to get rid of his dog?

he's old and he smells ☐   Candy has a new puppy ☐   Slim tells Carlson to ☐

c) What does Whit want to show Slim?

his gun ☐   a letter in a magazine ☐   a card trick ☐

d) Who reveals that he has three hundred dollars saved that he can put towards starting a farm?

George ☐   Whit ☐   Candy ☐

e) What does Lennie break when he grabs Curley?

his arm ☐   his hand ☐   his neck ☐

THINKING MORE DEEPLY ?

❷ Write **one** or **two sentences** in response to each of these questions:

a) What explanation does George give Slim for why he and Lennie had to leave Weed?

....

....

....

....

b) Why is Whit so excited about the magazine and Bill Tenner?

....

....

....

....

c) Why does Curley pick on Lennie?

....

....

....

....

....

EXAM PREPARATION: WRITING ABOUT THE SHOOTING OF CANDY'S DOG

Re-read the section from *'He led the dog out into the darkness.'* (p. 53) to *'Then he rolled slowly over and faced the wall and lay silent.'* (p. 54)

Question: How does Steinbeck create atmosphere and tension in this passage?

Think about:

- The language he uses to describe the setting and mood
- The way the men speak and behave

❸ Complete this table:

Point/detail	Evidence	Effect or explanation
1: *Steinbeck repeats key phrases or ideas.*	*'The silence came into the room' and 'The silence fell on the room again.'*	*The repetition of the reference to the silence builds tension as we await the gun-shot.*
2: *The men are shown to be edgy and uncomfortable with what is about to happen.*		
3: *Candy's reaction to what is happening shows how he is feeling.*		

❹ Write up **point 1** up into a **paragraph** below in your own words:

....

....

....

....

....

....

❺ Now, choose **one** of your **other points** and write it out as another **paragraph** here:

....

....

....

....

....

....

....

PROGRESS LOG [tick the correct box]   Needs more work ☐   Getting there ☐   Under control ☐

Section Four: Strange meeting

QUICK TEST ✔

❶ Which of these are **TRUE** statements about this section, and which are **FALSE**?
Write **'T'** or **'F'** into the boxes:

a) Crooks lives by himself in the harness room. ☐

b) George and the other men, except for Candy and Lennie, have gone into town. ☐

c) Crooks tells Lennie he comes from the south, not from California. ☐

d) Candy reveals it is the first time he has been into Crooks's room. ☐

e) Curley's wife believes Candy's explanation for Curley's broken hand. ☐

f) Curley's wife threatens Crooks when he says he is going to speak to the boss about her. ☐

g) Crooks tells Candy that he doesn't really want to join them on their farm. ☐

THINKING MORE DEEPLY ?

❶ Write **one** or **two sentences** in response to each of these questions:

a) In what ways is Crooks isolated from the other men on the ranch?

....

....

....

....

b) Why do you think that Curley's wife comes to the harness room (other than to look for Curley)?

....

....

....

....

c) Why do you think Steinbeck creates a scene such as this before the final, dramatic ending of the novel?

....

....

....

....

EXAM PREPARATION: WRITING ABOUT CROOKS AND HIS ROOM

Re-read the section from *'On one side of the little room ...'* (p. 73) to *'... pain-tightened lips which were lighter than his face.'* (p. 74)

Question: How does Steinbeck present Crooks in this passage?

Think about:

- The room and Crooks's possessions
- Crooks's appearance

❷ Complete this table:

Point/detail	Evidence	Effect or explanation
1: *Crooks is shown to be a skilful and important worker.*	*'... a little bench for leather-working tools ...'* *'... balls of linen thread, and a small hand riveter.'*	*These delicate items suggest dexterity of movement, and an eye for detail which others on the ranch might not possess.*
2: *He is presented as being well educated and as having more personal possessions than the other men.*		
3: *Steinbeck suggests he is a proud, almost heroic figure.*		

❸ Write up **point 1** into a **paragraph** below in your own words:

....

....

....

....

....

....

❹ Now, choose **one** of your **other points** and write it out as another **paragraph** here:

....

....

....

....

....

PROGRESS LOG [tick the correct box]   Needs more work ☐   Getting there ☐   Under control ☐

Section Five: Murder by mistake

QUICK TEST ✓

1 Which of these are **TRUE** statements about this section, and which are **FALSE**?
Write **'T'** or **'F'** into the boxes:

a) Lennie has brought a gun with him into the barn. ☐

b) Lennie is reluctant to talk to Curley's wife at first. ☐

c) Curley's wife asks Lennie to stroke her velvet dress. ☐

d) Lennie kills Curley's wife because she was going to tell everyone
about the puppy. ☐

e) Candy is the first person to find Curley's wife's body. ☐

f) The scene ends with a manhunt being organised. ☐

THINKING MORE DEEPLY ?

2 Write **one** or **two sentences** in response to each of these questions:

a) In what ways is Curley's wife unhappy with her life?

....

....

....

b) Why does Lennie end up killing Curley's wife?

....

....

....

c) What does George mean when he says, 'I think I knowed we'd never do her'
(p. 103)?

....

....

....

EXAM PREPARATION: WRITING ABOUT CURLEY'S WIFE

Re-read the section from *'Her face grew angry'* (p. 95) to *'... and her little finger stuck out grandly from the rest'* (p. 97).

Question: How do the details in this passage add to your understanding of Curley's wife?

Think about:

- What she says and does in this extract

❸ Complete this table:

Point/detail	Evidence	Effect or explanation
1: She wants to make conversation with someone who will listen to her.	She asks questions like 'Ain't I got a right to talk to nobody?'	She feels upset that she is controlled and silenced by most of the men on the ranch.
2: We find out about her dreams of stardom when she was younger.		
3: The description of her in death suggests there is an innocent side to her too.		

❹ Write up **point 1** into a **paragraph** below in your own words:

....

....

....

....

....

....

❺ Now, choose **one** of your **other points** and write it out as another **paragraph** here:

....

....

....

....

....

....

....

PROGRESS LOG [tick the correct box]　　Needs more work ☐　　Getting there ☐　　Under control ☐

Section Six: The end of the dream

QUICK TEST ✔

❶ Choose the **correct** answer to finish the statement and **tick** the box:

a) Lennie waits for George …

in the clearing by the pool ☐   in the harness room ☐   outside the bunk house ☐

b) Before George arrives, Lennie has an imaginary conversation with …

the dead puppy ☐   Aunt Clara and a giant rabbit ☐   George ☐

c) Lennie's first question when George appears is …

'You ain't gonna leave me, are ya, George?' ☐   'Is she dead?' ☐
'Did I do a bad thing?' ☐

d) When George hears the men getting really close, he tells Lennie to …

stand up ☐   run and hide in the brush ☐   take off his hat ☐

THINKING MORE DEEPLY ?

❷ Write **one** or **two sentences** in response to each of these questions:

a) How does George keep Lennie from turning around?

....

....

....

....

....

b) Do you think Lennie knew what George was going to do? Give reasons for your answer.

....

....

....

....

....

c) Why does Slim spend time talking to George after George has killed Lennie?

....

....

....

....

EXAM PREPARATION: WRITING ABOUT SETTING AND THEMES

Re-read the section from '*The deep green pool of the Salinas River …*' (p. 109) to '*… and laid his chin on his knees.*' (p. 110)

Question: How does Steinbeck's return to this setting add to our understanding of some of the key themes in the novel?

Think about:

- The setting

- Lennie's appearance and behaviour

❸ Complete this table:

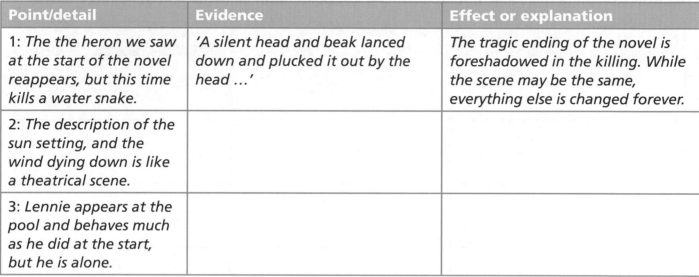

Point/detail	Evidence	Effect or explanation
1: *The the heron we saw at the start of the novel reappears, but this time kills a water snake.*	'*A silent head and beak lanced down and plucked it out by the head …*'	*The tragic ending of the novel is foreshadowed in the killing. While the scene may be the same, everything else is changed forever.*
2: *The description of the sun setting, and the wind dying down is like a theatrical scene.*		
3: *Lennie appears at the pool and behaves much as he did at the start, but he is alone.*		

❹ Write up **point 1** into a **paragraph** below in your own words:

....

....

....

....

....

❺ Now, choose **one** of your **other points** and write it out as another **paragraph** here:

....

....

....

....

....

PROGRESS LOG [tick the correct box]   Needs more work ☐   Getting there ☐   Under control ☐

Practice task

❶ First, **read** this **exam-style** task:

Read the section from *'Both men glanced up …'* (top of p. 34) to *'I never meant no harm, George. Honest I never.'* (p. 35) in Section Two.

Question: In this passage, what methods does Steinbeck use to present characters and events? Refer closely to the passage in your answer.

❷ Begin by circling the **key words** in the **question** above.

❸ Now, complete this table, noting down **3–4 key points** with **evidence** and the **effect** created:

Point	Evidence/quotation	Meaning or effect

❹ **Draft your response**. Use the space below for your first paragraph(s) and then continue onto a sheet of paper.

Start: *In this extract, Steinbeck presents both characters and events. Firstly, he introduces the reader to Curley's wife …*

....

....

....

....

....

....

....

....

....

....

PROGRESS LOG [tick the correct box]   Needs more work ☐   Getting there ☐   Under control ☐

PART THREE: CHARACTERS

Slim

❶ Look at these statements about Slim and decide whether they are **True** [T], **False** [F] or whether there is **Not Enough Evidence** [NEE] to make a decision.

a) Slim is a jerkline skinner who has responsibility for a team of mules. [T] [F] [NEE]

b) Slim refuses to give a puppy to Lennie. [T] [F] [NEE]

c) Slim supports Carlson's idea that Candy's dog should be killed. [T] [F] [NEE]

d) Slim comes up with the idea that Curley's hand was trodden
on by a horse. [T] [F] [NEE]

e) Slim is in favour of Candy, Lennie and George's plan to get a farm. [T] [F] [NEE]

f) Slim is sympathetic towards George when he kills Lennie. [T] [F] [NEE]

g) We do not know how old Slim is. [T] [F] [NEE]

❷ Complete each of these **statements** about Slim, using **your own words**:

a) *Slim has an important role in the novel as he …* ....

....

b) *The description of Slim when he first appears makes him seem like …* ....

....

c) *The way he deals with Curley's broken hand and makes Curley promise not to
tell on Lennie suggests that …* ....

....

d) *Slim listens carefully to what others have to say, for example when …* ....

....

e) *This tells the reader that …* ....

....

❸ Using your **own judgement**, put a mark along the line to show *your* attitude towards Slim based on what you have read:

Not at all sympathetic	A little sympathetic	Quite sympathetic	Very sympathetic
❶	❷	❸	❹

PROGRESS LOG [tick the correct box]   Needs more work ☐   Getting there ☐   Under control ☐

George

❶ Without checking the book, write down from memory at least **two bits of information** we are told about George in each of these areas:

His life and background	1: 2:
His appearance and looks	1: 2:
His behaviour and how he speaks	1: 2:

❷ Now **check your facts**. Are you right? Look at the following pages:

Life/background: Section Three (pp. 43–5)

Appearance and looks: Section One (p. 2), Section Two (p. 40)

His behaviour and how he speaks: with Lennie (Section One, pp. 3–7, Section Three, pp. 68–70), with Slim (Section Three, pp. 43–5), with Candy and the boss (Section Two, pp.19–25).

❸ Do you think George really **wants** to be with Lennie? Sort the **evidence** below into 'For' and 'Against' by ticking the appropriate column(s). **Think carefully** – some evidence could prove either viewpoint.

Evidence	For	Against
a) He promises Aunt Clara he'll look after Lennie.		
b) He mistreated Lennie when he was younger, but then realises how bad he's been.		
c) He finds work for him and Lennie together.		
d) He shouts at Lennie and tells him he could have a much easier life without him.		
e) He goes to the brothel, leaving Lennie behind.		
f) He shoots Lennie.		
g) He speaks for Lennie in most situations.		
h) He helps Lennie escape from Weed.		

PROGRESS LOG [tick the correct box]   Needs more work ☐   Getting there ☐   Under control ☐

Lennie

❶ Each of these qualities could be applied to Lennie. Working from **memory** add points in the story when you think these are shown, then find at least one **quotation** to back up your ideas.

Quality	Moment/s in story	Quotation
a) Child-like		
b) Frightened		
c) Powerful		
d) Cunning		
e) Angry		

❷ Which of these other **adjectives** would you add to the list? Circle them, and think of **one reason why**.

optimistic	innocent	comical	murderous	clumsy	cruel
fragile	cold	loyal	anxious	simple	

❸ Look at this quotation about Lennie. Add **further annotations** to it, using some of the **adjectives** above to show the effect:

He lifted her arm and let it drop. For a moment he <u>seemed bewildered.</u> And then he <u>whispered in fright,</u> 'I <u>done a bad thing. I done another bad thing.'</u>

Childlike language, shows his *simplicity*

Candy

❶ Look at these **statements** about Candy and then **circle** the ones that are **True** [T]
False [F] or for which there is **Not Enough Evidence** [NEE].

a) Candy is a 'swamper' or cleaner on the ranch. [T] [F] [NEE]

b) Candy lost his left hand in an accident. [T] [F] [NEE]

c) Candy is the first person George and Lennie meet when they
arrive. [T] [F] [NEE]

d) Candy is going to take one of the puppies to replace his old dog
when it is killed. [T] [F] [NEE]

e) Candy is keen to join George and Lennie in their plan to get a farm. [T] [F] [NEE]

f) Candy likes Crooks and thinks he should be allowed to stay with
the men in the bunk house. [T] [F] [NEE]

g) Candy blames Curley's wife for the end of the dream. [T] [F] [NEE]

❷ Complete these **statements** about Candy:

a) *We can make a comparison between Candy and his dog because ...* ....

....

b) *We can tell Candy is upset when the dog is shot from the way he ...* ....

....

c) *Candy's offer of his money for the farm is important because ...* ....

....

d) *When Curley's wife comes into Crooks's room, Candy stands up
to her which shows ...* ....

❸ Write **two sentences** saying what you think will happen to Candy in the future:

....

....

....

Using your **own judgement**, put a mark along the line to show **Steinbeck's attitude**
towards Candy based on what you have read:

Not at all sympathetic	A little sympathetic	Quite sympathetic	Very sympathetic
①	②	③	④

PROGRESS LOG [tick the correct box]   Needs more work ☐   Getting there ☐   Under control ☐

Curley

❶ Who says? Circle the character who makes these statements about, or to, Curley:

a) 'I don't *like* Curley. He ain't a nice fella.' (p. 97)

Curley's wife   George   Lennie   Candy

b) 'He spends half the time lookin' for her, and the rest of the time she's lookin' for him.' (p. 58)

Carlson   Whit   the boss   Slim

c) 'You come for me, an' I'll kick your God damn head off.' (p. 68)

Slim   Lennie   George   Carlson

d) 'I didn't wanta hurt him.' (p. 70)

Lennie   Curley's wife   George   Slim

e) 'Don't shoot 'im. He di'n't know what he was doin'.' (p. 107)

Slim   Candy   George   Whit

❷ Write **two sentences** in response to each of these questions:

a) In your opinion, who is more to blame for the death of Curley's wife – Curley or Lennie? Why?

....
....
....
....
....

b) What is Curley's reaction to his wife's death when he sees her in the barn?

....
....
....
....
....

c) 'Steinbeck presents Curley in a completely bad light': give your views on this statement:

....
....
....
....
....

PROGRESS LOG [tick the correct box]   Needs more work ☐   Getting there ☐   Under control ☐

Curley's wife

❶ Look at this bank of **adjectives** describing Curley's wife. Circle the ones you think best **describe** her:

cruel	bored	stupid	innocent	kind	flirtatious
thoughtful	friendly	lonely	desperate	cold	violent
	motherly	child-like	humorous	beautiful	

❷ Now add the **page reference** from your copy of the book next to each circle, showing where evidence can be found to **support** the **adjective**.

❸ Complete this **gap-fill paragraph** about Curley's wife, adding the **correct information**:

Curley's wife is never given a .... which adds to the feeling that we only see her through men's eyes. She first appears when she comes into the .... pretending to look for Curley. George warns Lennie to keep away from her, and calls her 'jail-bait' which suggests she could lead him into .... Later, George says the .... isn't a suitable place for a young woman with so many men around. If we judge solely by what the men say, it is clear they think she is always .... with them when Curley isn't around. However, when she talks with .... in the barn, a different side of her comes out; here she seems more vulnerable and seems to want companionship.

❹ Using your **own judgement**, put a mark along this line to show **Steinbeck's overall presentation** of Curley's wife:

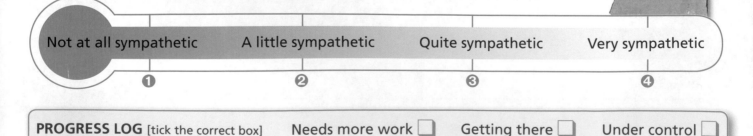

Not at all sympathetic	A little sympathetic	Quite sympathetic	Very sympathetic
❶	❷	❸	❹

PROGRESS LOG [tick the correct box]   Needs more work ☐   Getting there ☐   Under control ☐

Crooks

❶ **Complete** these **quotations** describing Crooks, or said by him.

a) 'Got a crooked back where a .... kicked him.' (p. 22)

b) 'I ain't wanted in the bunk house [...] 'Cause I'm ....' (p. 75)

c) 'And he had books, too; a tattered .... and a mauled copy of the California .... for 1905.' (p. 73)

d) 'He kept his .... and demanded that other people kept theirs.' (p. 74)

e) 'Nobody never gets to ...., and nobody gets no land.' (p. 81)

❷ Write a **paragraph** explaining **how Steinbeck presents** Crooks. Try to use one of the **quotations** above, or one of your own to **support** what you say:

I believe Steinbeck wants to present Crooks as ... .

....

....

....

....

....

....

....

....

....

Minor characters

❶ Don't forget the minor characters – the boss, Carlson and Whit. Read the descriptions and **circle the correct** character's name next to the description.

a) Who is 'a powerful big-stomached man'?   Carlson / Whit / the boss

b) Who 'wore high-heeled boots and spurs to prove he was not a labouring man'?   Carlson / Whit / the boss

c) Who 'did not surrender his hold' on his magazine, which contains a letter from a former ranch-hand?   Carlson / Whit / the boss

PROGRESS LOG [tick the correct box]   Needs more work ☐   Getting there ☐   Under control ☐

Practice task

❶ First, **read** this **exam-style** task:

Read the passage from Section Four, from *'They swung their heads toward the door ...'* (p. 84) to *'...an' likin' it because they ain't nobody else.'* (p. 86)
Question: How does Steinbeck present Curley's wife in this extract?

❷ Begin by circling the **key words** in the **question** above.

❸ Now, complete this table, noting down **3–4 key points** with **evidence** and the **effect** created:

Point	Evidence/quotation	Meaning or effect

❹ **Draft your response**. Use the space below for your first paragraph(s) and then continue onto a sheet of paper.

Start: *In this extract, Steinbeck presents Curley's wife in different ways. Firstly, he presents her as ...*

....

....

....

....

....

....

....

....

....

....

....

....

PROGRESS LOG [tick the correct box]   Needs more work ☐   Getting there ☐   Under control ☐

Key contexts

QUICK TEST

❶ Complete each statement, choosing the best response:

'The American Dream' refers to:

   a) Lennie's dream about his Aunt Clara at the end of the novel when she appears and tells him off

   b) The way in which America was seen as a place in which everyone was born equal and had the right to aspire to a better life, whatever their background

   c) The original title of the novel before it was called *Of Mice and Men*

   d) Candy's memories of his old dog and how long they have been together

❷ Complete the quotation from the Robert Burns poem, from which the title for *Of Mice and Men* comes: 'The best laid schemes o' mice and men, / gang aft agley [often go wrong] and ...':

   a) 'leave us nought but grief and pain / for promised joy!'

   b) 'keep us warm and cheered at night / till morning comes.'

   c) 'leave no trace when daylight comes / nor any joy.'

   d) 'make us dream of better life / with friends around.'

THINKING MORE DEEPLY

❸ Write **one** or **two sentences** in response to each of these questions:

   a) How did the Wall Street Crash affect workers such as George and Lennie?

   ....

   ....

   ....

   b) In what ways is the novel's title significant? (think about certain characters)

   ....

   ....

   ....

   c) Why do you think Steinbeck chose to set the novel in one location (even the pool is fairly close to the ranch)?

   ....

   ....

   ....

PROGRESS LOG [tick the correct box]   Needs more work ☐   Getting there ☐   Under control ☐

Key themes

QUICK TEST

❶ Circle the **themes** you think are most **relevant** to *Of Mice and Men*:

human fragility	love	marriage	fathers and sons
racial prejudice	nature	dreams and reality	country life	money
loneliness	ambition	hope	friendship	despair	violence

THINKING MORE DEEPLY

❷ Now choose the **three most important** of these and explain your **reasons in your own words**:

Theme 1: I think Steinbeck wanted to explore the theme of:

....

because ... .

....

....

....

Theme 2: I think Steinbeck wanted to explore the theme of:

....

because ... .

....

....

....

Theme 3: I think Steinbeck wanted to explore the theme of:

....

because ... .

....

....

....

❸ It's important you use **quotations** to **explain themes**. Read this quotation from Crooks and then:

- Write down which theme(s) it represents
- Add further comments to explain or make links

'Ever'body wants a <u>little piece of lan'</u>. I read plenty of books out here. <u>Nobody never gets to heaven,</u> and <u>nobody gets no land</u>. <u>It's just in their head'</u>. (p. 81)

despair

Very pessimistic view; not surprising coming from Crooks, who is in pain and an outsider

❹ Some events in the novel seem to link to particular themes rather than having an actual effect on the plot. What **themes** do these **events** link to?

a) *George catching Lennie with a dead mouse at the start of the novel*

Links to theme(s) of: ....

Why … ....

....

b) *The shooting of Candy's dog*

Links to theme(s) of: ....

Why … ....

....

c) *The game of cards in the bunk house*

Links to theme(s) of: ....

Why … ....

....

d) *Whit seeing that one of the ex-ranch hands has a letter in the magazine*

Links to theme(s) of: ....

Why … ....

....

PROGRESS LOG [tick the correct box]   Needs more work ☐   Getting there ☐   Under control ☐

Practice task

❶ First, **read** this **exam-style** task:

Question: In the novel as a whole, in what ways does Steinbeck present the idea of life being fragile?

❷ Begin by circling the **key words** in the **question** above.

❸ Now, complete this table, noting down **3–4 key points** with **evidence** and the **effect** created:

Point	Evidence/quotation	Meaning or effect

❹ **Draft your response**. Use the space below for your first paragraph(s) and then continue onto a sheet of paper.

Start: *In the novel, Steinbeck presents the idea of the fragility of life in a range of ways. Firstly, we see ...*

PROGRESS LOG [tick the correct box]   Needs more work ☐   Getting there ☐   Under control ☐

Language

❶ Match these **literary terms** to **examples** of them **from the novel**:

Term	Example
symbol	'... a manure pile under the window. Sure, it's swell.' (p. 82; Crooks, about his hut)
imagery	'Lennie dabbled his big paw in the water.' (p. 3)
irony	Dreams and reality
colloquial	Lennie kills Curley's wife, but could be said to be 'innocent'
theme	Candy's old dog represents companionship
paradox	'An' you ain't gonna do no bad things like you done in Weed, neither.' (p. 7; George to Lennie)

Two sorts of **imagery** are **simile** and **metaphor**:

● **Simile**: when you say one thing is *like* another.

● **Metaphor**: when you describe one thing as if it *really were* something else; you don't use 'like' or 'as'.

❷ For each of the **quotations** below, circle the **correct response**: **S** (simile), **M** (metaphor) or **N** (neither)

a)	'The low horizontal limb of a giant sycamore tree ...' (p. 1)	S	M	N
b)	'... snorting into the water like a horse.' (p. 2; about Lennie)	S	M	N
c)	'The sycamore leaves whispered in a little night breeze.' (p. 18)	S	M	N
d)	'A solid door with a wooden latch ...' (p. 19)	S	M	N
e)	'You're as yella as a frog belly ...' (p. 68; Carlson to Curley)	S	M	N

THINKING MORE DEEPLY

❸ Now choose **one simile** and **one metaphor** and in your own words **explain** the **effect** of Steinbeck using them:

Steinbeck uses **a simile** to describe ....

The effect of this is ....

....

He uses **a metaphor** to describe ....

The effect of this is ....

....

❹ Read these examples of **similes** and then **decide** which of the **explanations** below is the most important. **Rate each explanation** by circling **1** (least important), **2** (quite important) or **3** (most important).

a) *Steinbeck's simile which describes Curley 'flopping like a fish on a line' (p. 69) is particularly effective because ...*

... he is in pain and under Lennie's control   1   2   3

... it has lots of 'f' sounds in it so is memorable   1   2   3

... it shows Curley's desperate movements to break free   1   2   3

Can you think of any other reason why this is such a well-chosen simile?

It is also well chosen because ... .

....

....

....

b) *Steinbeck describes George's face as being 'as hard and as tight as wood' (p. 102) when he finds Curley's wife's body. This is particularly effective because ...*

... it suggests how George will have to be cold and strong
on the outside, even if he feels emotional inside.   1   2   3

... they are on a ranch, and wood is a common texture.   1   2   3

... George is a tough person.   1   2   3

Can you think of any other reason why this is such a well-chosen simile?

It is also well chosen because ... .

....

....

....

QUICK TEST

Steinbeck uses a small number of well-chosen details to make scenes vivid as we read them.

⑤ Read these quotations from the novel and then **tick the box** (or boxes) to **indicate** which of the **five senses** Steinbeck is **referring** to:

Quotation	sight	taste	sound	touch or texture	smell
a) ' ... the sun threw a bright dust-laden bar through one of the side windows ...' (p.19)					
b) '... he rubbed his bristly white whiskers with his knuckles.' (p. 21)					
c) ' ...the thuds and occasional clangs of a horseshoe game ...' (p. 42)					
d) '... a drippy can of tar with its paint brush sticking over the edge.' (p. 73)					
e) 'They ... filled their mouths with beans and chewed mightily.' (p. 16)					
f) ' ...the leaves rustled ... And the shouts of the men sounded again, this time much closer than before.' (p. 114)					
g) '... she caught the dead scent of Curley's wife, and the hair rose along her spine.' (p. 101)					

⑥ Which of the following scenes from the novel do **you** find it **easiest to picture** in your mind? Rate each scene 1–5 (1 being 'the least' to 5 being 'the most').

a) Lennie by the pool at the start of the novel (pp. 2–3)   1   2   3   4   5

b) The description of the bunk house (p. 19)   1   2   3   4   5

c) The description of Curley's wife (p. 34)   1   2   3   4   5

d) Crooks's room (p. 73)   1   2   3   4   5

e) Curley's wife's story about her past (p. 96)   1   2   3   4   5

THINKING MORE DEEPLY

⑦ Now, select one of the scenes in task 6 and **write two sentences** explaining how **you** think Steinbeck makes it vivid and brings it to life:

....

....

....

PROGRESS LOG [tick the correct box]   Needs more work ☐   Getting there ☐   Under control ☐

Structure

❶ To understand the structure of *Of Mice and Men*, it can be helpful to compare it to a play – like a play, it has a precise structure. In what other ways is *Of Mice and Men* similar to a play? Choose **Not similar** [NS], **Similar** [S] or **Very similar** [VS] for each of these statements:

a) There are a series of 'scenes', which follow on from each other, building tension.	NS	S	VS
b) We are told characters' thoughts, without them being spoken out loud.	NS	S	VS
c) Each scene has a clearly identifiable setting.	NS	S	VS
d) There is a lot of dialogue and speech.	NS	S	VS
e) There are several very dramatic scenes.	NS	S	VS
f) It has a small number of characters.	NS	S	VS

❷ There are lots of clues which **foreshadow** the ending. Can you put them in the **(time) order** in which they happen? Number the events below **1** to **6** (1 for the first event; 6 for the last event).

a) Lennie's killing of mice ☐

b) What happened between Lennie and the girl in Weed ☐

c) The shooting of Candy's dog ☐

d) The killing of the puppy ☐

e) Curley's wife's interest in Lennie when she comes to Crooks's room ☐

f) The fight with Curley showing Lennie's vast strength ☐

❸ How inevitable do **you** think the tragedy was? Circle your choice and then write a paragraph explaining why.

Not at all   Partly   Quite   Very

Why? ....

....

....

....

....

....

....

PROGRESS LOG [tick the correct box]   Needs more work ☐   Getting there ☐   Under control ☐

Practice task

❶ First, **read** this **exam-style** task:

Read from the beginning of Section Two to *'Used to wash his hands even* after *he ate.'* (p. 20)

Question: How does Steinbeck use language to present a vivid impression of the bunk house and Candy?

❷ Begin by circling the **key words** in the **question** above.

❸ Now, complete this table, noting down **3–4 key points** with **evidence** and the **effect** created:

Point	Evidence/quotation	Meaning or effect

❹ **Draft your response**. Use the space below for your first paragraph(s) and then continue onto a sheet of paper.

Start: *In the novel, Steinbeck describes the bunk house vividly in a range of ways. Firstly, he ...*

....
....
....
....
....
....
....
....
....
....
....

PROGRESS LOG [tick the correct box]   Needs more work ☐   Getting there ☐   Under control ☐

Writing skills

❶ How well can you express your ideas about *Of Mice and Men*? Look at this grid, and tick the **level** you think you are **currently** at:

Level	How you respond	What your spelling, punctuation and grammar is like	Tick
Higher	• You analyse the effect of specific words and phrases very closely (i.e. 'zooming in' on them and exploring their meaning). • You select quotations very carefully and you embed them fluently in your sentences. • You are persuasive and convincing in the points you make, often coming up with original ideas.	• You use a wide range of specialist terms (words like 'imagery'), excellent punctuation, accurate spelling, grammar, etc.	
Mid	• You analyse some parts of the text closely, but not all the time. • You support what you say with evidence and quotations, but sometimes your writing could be more fluent to read. • You make relevant comments on the text.	• You use a good range of specialist terms, generally accurate punctuation and usually accurate spelling, grammar, etc.	
Lower	• You comment on some words and phrases but often you do not develop your ideas. • You sometimes use quotations to back up what you say but they are not always well chosen. • You mention the effect of certain words and phrases but these are not always relevant to the task.	• You do not have a very wide range of specialist terms, but you use reasonably accurate spelling, punctuation and grammar.	

SELECTING AND USING QUOTATIONS

❷ Read these two samples from students' responses to a question about how Lennie is presented in Section Four. Decide which of the three levels they fit best, i.e. **lower** (L), **mid** (M) or **higher** (H).

Student A: *Lennie shows his friendly nature when he visits Crooks. He 'smiled helplessly in an attempt to make friends'. This shows that he doesn't know how to act around people.*

Level ? ☐ Why? ....

....

Student B: *Steinbeck presents Lennie as awkward in his dealings with others as shown in the way he 'smiled helplessly in an attempt to make friends'. The verb 'smiled' shows his desire to be liked but the adverb 'helplessly' suggests he really doesn't know how to.*

Level ? ☐ Why? ....

....

ZOOMING IN – YOUR TURN!

Here is the first part of another student response. The student has picked a good quotation but hasn't 'zoomed in' on any particular words or phrases:

When Crooks suggests that George might not come back, we see how quickly Lennie's friendliness can turn to anger, as his 'eyes centered and grew quiet, and mad'.

❸ Pick out one of the **words** or **phrases** the student has quoted and write a further **sentence** to complete the explanation, using your own words:

The word/phrase '..*' suggests that* ....

....

....

....

EXPLAINING IDEAS

You need to be precise about the way Steinbeck communicates his ideas. This can be achieved by varying your use of verbs (not just using 'says' or 'means').

❹ Read this paragraph from a **mid-level** response to the same task. Circle all the **verbs** that are repeated:

Steinbeck shows us that Lennie lacks understanding of the world when he says to Crooks, 'Why ain't you wanted?' This says that he doesn't understand prejudice. It also says that he doesn't understand himself or he would see that he is different too. This shows us that Crooks and he are linked, even if they don't see it.

❺ Now choose some of the words in the bank below to replace your circled ones:

suggests	implies	tells us	presents	signals	asks
	demonstrates	recognise	comprehend		

❻ Rewrite **your higher-level** version of the paragraph in full below. Remember to mention the **author by name** to show you understand he is **making choices** in how he presents characters, themes and events.

....

....

....

....

....

....

PROGRESS LOG [tick the correct box]   Needs more work ☐   Getting there ☐   Under control ☐

Spelling, punctuation and grammar

Here are a number of key words you might use when writing in the exam:

Content and structure	Characters and style	Linguistic features
section	character	imagery
paragraph	role	simile
quotation	protagonist	metaphor
sequence	dramatic	personification
dialogue	tragedy	juxtaposition
climax	villainous	irony
development	humorous	repetition
introduction	sympathetic	symbol

❶ Circle any you might find difficult to spell, and then use the 'Look, Say, Cover, Write, Check' method to learn them. This means: **look** at the word; **say** it out loud; then **cover** it up; **write** it out (without looking at it!); uncover and **check** your spelling with the correct version.

❷ Create a **mnemonic** for five of your difficult spellings. For example,

tragedy: **t**en **r**eally **a**ngry **g**irls **e**njoyed **d**ancing **y**esterday!   Or …

break the word down: T – RAGE – DY!

a) ....

b) ....

c) ....

d) ....

e) ....

❸ Circle any **incorrect spellings** in this paragraph and then rewrite it:

We see how Lenny is magnetised by Curly's wife when she comes into Crooks's room as it says he 'watched her, fascinated …'. The developement of this idea is an omen of the tragedie to come as it once again hilights her central roll in the novel, even though she's not the main protoganist.

....

....

....

....

❹ Punctuation can help make your meaning clear. Here is one response by a student commenting on Crooks's reaction to Curley's wife. Check for correct use of:

- Apostrophes
- Speech marks for quotations
- Full stops and commas

When Curleys wife threatens Crooks Steinbeck 'describes how he sat down on his bunk and drew into himself' this implies Crooks is like a wounded animal thats seeking shelter inside his shell and doesnt want to anger provoke or challenge it's tormentor.

Rewrite it **correctly** here:

....

....

....

....

....

❺ Watch for tenses. It is better to use the present tense to describe what is happening in the book.

Look at these two extracts. Which one **uses tenses consistently** and **accurately**?

Student A

Steinbeck had presented a very moving conclusion to the novel when George was forced to kill Lennie; George didn't have any choice. Steinbeck suggests the ending was inevitable.

Student B

Steinbeck presents a very moving conclusion to the novel when George is forced to kill Lennie; George doesn't have any choice. Steinbeck suggests the ending is inevitable.

❻ Now look at this further paragraph. **Underline** or **circle** all the **verb tenses** first.

Slim <u>had comforted</u> George and told him, 'Never you mind …' after he kills Lennie. This suggested that Slim was an understanding and decent person, the only one who will recognise George's dilemma.

Now rewrite it using the **present tense consistently**:

....

....

....

....

....

PROGRESS LOG [tick the correct box]   Needs more work ☐   Getting there ☐   Under control ☐

Planning and structure

STRUCTURE AND LINKING OF PARAGRAPHS

❶ Read this paragraph by a student who is explaining how Steinbeck presents Slim:

He says: 'There was a gravity in his manner and a quiet so profound that all talk stopped when he spoke.' This means that people listened to him. I think it means they respect him.

> **Expert viewpoint:** This paragraph isn't very logical. It doesn't begin with a clear topic sentence explaining how Steinbeck presents Slim. It also doesn't really explain or 'zoom in' on any of the key words.

Now, **rewrite** the paragraph in your own words. Start with a **topic sentence**, and pick out a **key phrase** or **word** to 'zoom in' on …

Steinbeck presents Slim as someone who … ....

....

....

....

....

....

❷ Read this paragraph by another student also commenting on how Slim is presented:

Steinbeck describes several elements of Slim's appearance. He says that his 'hatchet face was ageless'. This tells us his face is hard and sharp. It tells us it is not easy to say how old he was. He is almost like a statue. He mentions that his hands 'were as delicate in their action as those of a temple dancer'. There is something graceful about them.

> **Expert viewpoint:** There are some very good points here but the style is clumsy with very few of the sentences linked. There need to be joining words or phrases like 'for example', 'and', 'also' or 'furthermore' (for an additional point), 'which suggests …', 'which implies …', etc.

Rewrite the paragraph, **improving** the **style**, and also try to add a **concluding sentence summing up** Slim's appearance.

Start with the same opening topic sentence:

Steinbeck describes several elements of Slim's appearance. ....

....

....

....

....

....

PLANNING AN ESSAY

Read this **exam-style task**:

Question: _How_ does Steinbeck present ideas about isolation and loneliness in the novel?

❸ Select the key words in this question by underlining them or highlighting them. The first has been done for you.

❹ Write a simple **plan** with **five key points** (the first two have been done for you). Think about – Crooks, Curley's wife, the way the men live.

1) _Steinbeck shows that it is seen as strange for men to travel together._

2) _He describes Candy's need to keep his old dog._

3) ....

   ....

4) ....

   ....

5) ....

   ....

❺ Now list **five quotations, one** for each **point**: the first two have been provided for you.

1) _The boss (to George, about Lennie): 'Well, I never seen one guy take so much trouble for another guy. I just like to know what your interest is.' (p. 24)_

2) _'I'm so used to him,' he said softly. 'I had him from a pup.' (p. 49)_

3) ....

   ....

4) ....

   ....

5) ....

   ....

❻ Now read this task and **write a plan of your own**, including **quotations**, on a separate sheet of paper.

Read from 'Lennie said softly, "I di'n't forget, you bet ..."' (p. 110) to '... George ain't gonna let me tend no rabbits now.' (p. 111)

Question: _How does Steinbeck present Lennie in this section?_

PROGRESS LOG [tick the correct box]   Needs more work ☐   Getting there ☐   Under control ☐

Sample answers

OPENING PARAGRAPHS

Here is one of the tasks from the previous page:

Question: *How does Steinbeck present ideas about isolation and loneliness in the novel?*

Now look at these two alternative openings to the essay, and read the expert viewpoints underneath:

Student A

> *Steinbeck presents ideas about isolation and loneliness in a number of ways in the novel. The most obvious example of this is that there are characters like Candy and Crooks who are truly alone and find different ways to deal with it. But there are other characters who Steinbeck presents as isolated in other ways such as Curley's wife, and even characters such as Whit.*

Student B

> *George and Lennie would be isolated if they didn't have each other but luckily they do. But they are lonely by the end which is why Lennie wants to talk to Curley's wife and George has gone off into town with the other men. These are important themes because everyone is affected.*

Expert viewpoint 1: This is a good, clear paragraph which introduces some of the key characters which the student is going to discuss as part of his or her essay. The introduction suggests that there are different types of loneliness, and that characters have different ways of dealing with it. The student could have briefly made reference to Lennie and George.

Expert viewpoint 2: This introduction focuses solely on Lennie and George when it should really introduce the theme more generally, mentioning other aspects. It also describes a specific point in the text, something which would be better in the main body of the answer.

❶ Which comment belongs to which answer? Match the paragraph (A or B) to the expert feedback (1 or 2).

Student A: ....   Student B: ....

❷ Now it's your turn. Write the opening paragraph to this task on a separate sheet of paper:

Read from 'Lennie said softly, 'i di'n't forget, you bet ...' (p. 110) to '.... George ain't gonna let me tend no rabbits now.' (p. 111)

Question: *How does Steinbeck present Lennie in this extract?*

Remember:

● Introduce the topic in general terms, perhaps **explaining** or **'unpicking'** the key **words** or **ideas** in the task (such as 'present').

● Mention the **different possibilities** or ideas that you are going to address.

● Use the **author's name**.

WRITING ABOUT TECHNIQUES

Here are two paragraphs in response to a different task, where the students have focused on the writer's techniques. The task is:

Read from *'It was very quiet in the barn …'* to *'… for much, much more than a moment.'* (p. 101)

Question: *What methods does Steinbeck use to present Curley's wife in this passage?*

Student A

> The response of the dog to the death of Curley's wife shows that she is sympathetic. 'She caught the dead scent of Curley's wife, and the hair rose along her spine.' The puppy is also dead so this creates a connection between the innocent dead puppy and Curley's wife. This is effective as it changes our view of Curley's wife.

Student B

> Steinbeck provides a simple detail of the response of the dog to Curley's wife's body as 'she caught the dead scent'. This cleverly links her death to that of other innocent creatures such as the puppy, and reminds us that both Curley's wife and the puppy met their death at Lennie's hands. In addition, Steinbeck's juxtaposition of an animal and a human being, one alive, the other dead, connected through the word 'caught', suggests that human life is no more or less important than any other, all deserving our sympathy.

Expert viewpoint 1: This is a higher level paragraph which fluently expresses the importance of the dog's response. It comments on the specific event but also makes wider comments on key issues and ideas, using accurate literary terminology to do so. The final point is a little over complicated but shows an ambitious attempt to make links and focus in on key details.

Expert viewpoint 2: This is a mid level response which makes a clear point about Curley's wife and selects an appropriate quotation to support it. However, the quotation is not fluently embedded in the sentence and there is no real detailed analysis of it, although it does draw a connection between Curley's wife and the dead puppy. The final sentence feels unfinished.

❸ Which comment belongs to which answer? Match the paragraph (A or B) to the expert feedback (1 or 2).

Student A: ··· Student B: ···

❹ Now, take another aspect of the passage and write your own paragraph on a separate sheet of paper. You could comment on one of these aspects:

- The opening to the passage and how it sets the scene
- The description of Curley's wife as she lies in the hay
- The end of the passage when 'a moment' is described

Now read this longer, **lower-level** response to the following task:

Read from *'Lennie said softly, "I di'n't forget, you bet ..."'* (p. 110) to *'... George ain't gonna let me tend no rabbits now.'* (p. 111)

Question: *How does Steinbeck present Lennie in this section?*

Student response:

> *Lennie is back at the pool where the story began so the story has come full circle. Like everything was a waste of time and they have just gone backwards. Lennie is shown talking to himself and congratulating himself for remembering where to go. 'I di'n't forget, you bet ...'.   But then he says, 'George gonna give me hell.'*
>
> *Lennie is crazy as he sees Aunt Clara in his head and starts talking to her. The things she says back show that Lennie cares more about little things than the really bad things he has done. Also everything is mixed up as Aunt Clara says what George would say.*

Expert viewpoint: There are some good points here but the first paragraph doesn't really start to answer the question until the third sentence. The student needs to refer directly to 'Steinbeck' to make it clear what he is doing as an author. The first two quotations are well chosen but they are not analysed in much detail. The second paragraph is too informal and there is no supporting quotation. The expression could be better, too (for example, 'things' is repeated three times).

⑤ **Rewrite** these two paragraphs in your own words, **improving** them by **addressing**:

- The lack of development or linking of points – no 'zooming in' on key words or phrases
- The lack of quotations and embedding
- Unnecessary repetition, and poor use of specialist terms and vocabulary

Paragraph 1:

In this section, Steinbeck presents Lennie in a range of ways. Firstly, he ... .

....

This suggests that ... .

....

Furthermore ... .

....

Paragraph 2:

Steinbeck shows another side to Lennie when his Aunt Clara 'appears'. He ... .

....

This implies that ... .

....

This links with ... .

....

A FULL-LENGTH RESPONSE

⑥ Now, write a full-length response to this exam-style task on a separate sheet of paper. Answer both parts of the question:

Read from *'Slim moved back slightly...'* (p. 43) to *'Well, I ain't done nothing like that no more.'* (p. 44).

Part A

How does Steinbeck present George in this extract?

Part B

In the rest of the novel, how does Steinbeck present other characters who seek companionship and a chance to explain themselves?

- Plan **quickly** (no more than 5 minutes) what you intend to write, jotting down **4–5 supporting quotations**.

- Refer closely to the **key words** in the question.

- Make sure you comment on **what** the writer does, the **techniques** he uses and the **effect** of those techniques.

- Support your points with **well-chosen quotations** or other **evidence**.

- Develop your points by **'zooming-in'** on particular **words** or **phrases** and explaining their **effect**.

- Be **persuasive** and **convincing** in what you say

- Check carefully for **spelling, punctuation** and **grammar**.

PROGRESS LOG [tick the correct box]   Needs more work ☐   Getting there ☐   Under control ☐

Further questions

1. Read from *'George's voice became deeper ...'* (p. 14) to *'... How I get to tend the rabbits.'* (top of p. 16)

   How does Steinbeck present the relationship between George and Lennie here?

2. How does Steinbeck use animals to reflect some of the key themes in the novel as a whole?

3. Read from *'At that moment a young man came into the bunk house ...'* (p. 27) to *'... and his elbows were still bent out a little.'* (p. 28)

   How does Steinbeck present Curley in this extract?

4. How does Steinbeck use the character of Curley in the novel as a whole to explore the negative side of human relationships?

5. In what ways does Steinbeck explore the theme of dreams through the life of the ranch hands?

ANSWERS

NOTE: Answers have been provided for most tasks. Exceptions are 'Practice tasks' and tasks which ask you to write a paragraph or use your own words or judgement.

PART ONE: INTRODUCTION [pp. 6–7]

INTRODUCING OF MICE AND MEN

1. Setting

Weed: Where Lennie touched the girl's dress. Lennie and George flee from here; **Salinas River:** Novel opens and ends here; **Soledad:** Local town where ranch-hands 'blow off steam'; **Harness room:** Crooks's place. Where Lennie, Candy and Crooks talk until Curley's wife comes in; **The Bunk House:** Where the ranch hands sleep. Where Curley fights with Lennie; **The Barn:** Where the puppies and mother sleep. Lennie kills Curley's wife here; **The Homestead:** The boss's house. Curley and Curley's wife live here

2. Characters: Who's who

Top left: George and Lennie: two migrant workers; Bottom left: Carlson and Whit: workers on the ranch; Top middle: Crooks: stable hand; Bottom middle: Curley and his wife: boss's son and ex-boxer, and his new wife; Top right: Candy and his dog: an old man who cleans the ranch and his old sheepdog; Middle right: Slim: head of one of the grain teams; Bottom right: the boss: the man in charge of the ranch

3. John Steinbeck: Author and context

a) Salinas; b) university; c) Crash; d) novel; e) 1937; f) Second; g) Pulitzer; h) Literature; i) *East of Eden*

PART TWO: PLOT AND ACTION [pp. 8–19]

SECTION ONE: MOVING ON [pp. 8–9]

1.

a) a dead mouse; b) Lennie touched a girl's dress; c) to a ranch for work; d) buy a small farm and keep rabbits; e) return to the same pool

2.

a)
- George is small, has a sharp, 'defined' face and moves quickly.
- Lennie is large, with a 'shapeless' face, and has heavy movements.

b)
- A bear – 'dragging his feet a little, the way a bear drags its paws'.
- A horse – 'snorting into the water like a horse'.

c)
- They add to the rural, agricultural setting of the novel.
- They are an important element in Lennie's dream of having a farm, so could be seen as an omen.

3.

Point/detail	Evidence	Effect or explanation
1: *George looks out for Lennie and tells him what (or what not) to do.*	He uses commands such as: '... don't drink so much.'	*George behaves like a parent might to a small child who can't be trusted to make his own decisions.*
2: *Lennie behaves and speaks in a child-like way.*	'I ain't got nothing George.' (about the dead mouse) 'I like beans with ketchup.'	*Lennie takes pleasure in child-like activities, and denies wrong-doing. George sometimes disapproves or ignores Lennie's actions.*
3: *Lennie seeks George's approval.*	'Look, George. Look what I done.' (about making ripples) 'George, you want I should go away and leave you alone?'	*Lennie wants to make George happy, but is also cunning enough to know that George won't abandon him.*

SECTION TWO: RISING TENSIONS [pp. 10–11]

1.

b) = 1; c) = 2; a) = 3; e) = 4; g) = 5; d) = 6; f) = 7

2.

a)
- They didn't arrive when they were supposed to.
- He finds it strange that Lennie doesn't say much and that the two men are travelling together.

b)
- Curley is cold and aggressive.
- He is also angry and controlling (of his wife).

c)
- We see Curley's aggression, which will lead to the fight with Lennie.
- It shows Lennie's attraction to Curley's wife.

3.

Point/detail	Evidence	Effect or explanation
1: *The minimum effort has been made to make the place liveable.*	'... the walls were whitewashed and the floor unpainted.'	*The bunk house is very basic and functional, and reminds everyone that this is a place of work, rather than their own home.*
2: *There is little privacy for the men.*	'Against the wall were eight bunks ...'	*The men live right alongside each other, rather like soldiers in barracks.*
3: *Space for personal possessions does exist but it is very limited.*	'Over each bunk there was nailed an apple box with the opening forward so that it made two shelves ...'	*All the men have is this one makeshift area for their belongings, which can't be closed off.*

SECTION THREE: THE DAWN OF HOPE [pp. 12–13]

1.

a) Auburn; b) he's old and he smells; c) a letter in a magazine; d) Candy; e) his hand

2.

a)

- Lennie grabbed hold of a girl's dress and she went to the 'law' to say she'd been 'raped'.
- A group of men wanted to lynch Lennie so they had to hide and then leave.

b)

- Bill used to work at the ranch.
- It is a glamorous link to the outside world (in Whit's mind).

c)

- The other men stand up to him and aren't frightened.
- He thinks Lennie is laughing at him.

3.

Point/detail	Evidence	Effect or explanation
1: Steinbeck repeats key phrases or ideas	'The silence came into the room' and 'The silence fell on the room again.'	The repetition of the reference to the silence builds tension as we await the gun-shot.
2: The men are shown to be edgy and uncomfortable with what is about to happen.	'There came a little gnawing sound from under the floor and all the men looked down toward it gratefully.' 'What the hell's takin' him so long?' (Whit)	They are keen to be diverted from thinking about the shooting. They want the shooting to be over and done with.
3: Candy's reaction to what is happening shows how he is feeling.	'For a moment he continued to stare at the ceiling. Then he rolled slowly over and faced the wall and lay silent.'	Candy is isolated and turns his back on the men, implying how distressed he feels at what's happened.

SECTION FOUR: STRANGE MEETING [pp. 14–15]

1.

a) T; b) T; c) F; d) T; e) F; f) T; g) T

2.

a)

- His skin colour
- His job/role and where he lives/stays – in the harness room
- His education (he is more well-read)

b)

- She wants someone to talk to.
- She's fed up with Curley; he's not much of a husband.

c)

- It is a moment of peace and reflection before the big climax.
- It provides a wider picture of society and other types of prejudice and human weakness.

3.

Point/detail	Evidence	Effect or explanation
1: Crooks is shown to be a skilful and important worker.	'... a little bench for leather-working tools ...' '... balls of linen thread, and a small hand riveter.'	These delicate items suggest dexterity of movement, and an eye for detail which others on the ranch might not possess.
2: He is presented as being well educated and as having more personal possessions than the other men.	'a tattered dictionary' 'a mauled copy of the California civil code' 'large gold-rimmed spectacles'	A dictionary and a law book suggest a thirst for knowledge. The glasses – good ones – imply that in other circumstances Crooks might have had a profession such as teaching.
3: Steinbeck suggests he is a proud, almost heroic figure.	'his eyes lay deep in his head' '... seemed to glitter with intensity' 'pain-tightened lips'	Suggests he has hidden depths, which he cannot show. Suggests that he has power or passion waiting to be unleashed. He does not complain about his pain but it is always with him.

SECTION FIVE: MURDER BY MISTAKE [pp. 16–17]

1.

a) F; b) T; c) F; d) F; e) T; f) T

2.

a)

- Curley gets jealous if she talks to anyone but him. This makes her isolated and lonely.
- She believes she could have had a more glamorous life as an actress.

b)

- He tries to stop Curley's wife screaming when he holds onto her hair.
- He gets angry when she struggles and breaks her neck by shaking her.

c)

- He knew all along that the dream of the farm was a fantasy.
- Perhaps he had gone along with it to keep Lennie happy.

3.

Point/detail	Evidence	Effect or explanation
1: She wants to make conversation with someone who will listen to her.	She asks questions like 'Ain't I got a right to talk to nobody?'	She feels upset that she is controlled and silenced by most of the men on the ranch.
2: We find out about her dreams of stardom when she was younger.	'... he was gonna put me in the movies. Says I was a natural.'	She believes, falsely, that she was going to get a letter inviting her to Hollywood; it's another fantasy that has little basis in reality.
3: The description of her in death suggests there is an innocent side to her too.	'... the meanness and the plannings and the discontent and the ache for attention were all gone from her face.' '... her face was sweet and young.'	With Lennie she seems to be quite child-like and simple; once she is dead this is further emphasised by the description of her as untroubled by the worries of the world, or how she could get attention.

SECTION SIX: THE END OF THE DREAM [pp. 18–19]

1.

a) in the clearing by the pool; b) Aunt Clara and a giant rabbit; c) 'You ain't gonna leave me, are ya, George?'; d) take off his hat

2.

a)
- He says he'll tell him about their dream of having a farm.
- He tells him to look across the river so he can actually 'see' it.

b)
- Yes – surely Lennie would have heard the shouts of the men who were after him? Also he knows what a bad thing he has done.
- No – Lennie is still just as eager to hear about the dream of having a farm; he trusts George completely, too.

c)
- To comfort him.
- To persuade him that he had no choice but to kill Lennie.

3.

Point/detail	Evidence	Effect or explanation
1: The heron we saw at the start of the novel reappears, but this time kills a water snake.	'A silent head and beak lanced down and plucked it out by the head …'	The tragic ending of the novel is foreshadowed in the killing. While the scene may be the same, everything else is changed forever.
2: The description of the sun setting, and the wind dying down is like a theatrical scene.	'… the wind died, and the clearing was quiet again.'	This is like the curtains opening as the music fades and the actor (Lennie) enters.
3: Lennie appears at the pool and behaves in much as he did at the start, but he is alone.	'… came as silently as a creeping bear moves.' '… knelt down and drank, barely touching his lips to the water.'	Lennie is presented as almost at one with nature. He drinks quietly this time, as if conscious that things have changed; he is a bear who is now being hunted down.

PART THREE: CHARACTERS [pp. 21–7]

SLIM [p. 21]

1.

a) T; b) F; c) T; d) F; e) NEE; f) T; g) T

2.

a) Slim has an important role in the novel as he **provides support to George and makes key decisions, such as about Candy's dog and Curley's hand.**

b) The description of Slim when he first appears makes him seem like **a king or a monarch, or even a wise and deep philosopher, almost god-like.**

c) The way he deals with Curley's broken hand and makes Curley promise not to tell on Lennie suggests that he **has authority and is respected, and that he has sympathy for Lennie.**

d) Slim listens carefully to what others have to say, for example when **he first meets George and Lennie, and George tells him about his background and what happened in Weed.**

e) This tells the reader that **Slim is someone whom people feel they can trust and confide in. He has the respect of the ranch, and is considered a leader.**

GEORGE [p. 22]

1.

His life and background	1: Comes from Auburn
	2: Used to make fun of Lennie
His appearance and looks	1: Small with slim arms, 'restless' eyes
	2: Sharp features, thin and bony nose
His behaviour and how he speaks	1: Quick in his movements, sums people up rapidly
	2: Sometimes irritable (with Lennie), also cautious when explaining situations

3.

a) For – but it may also be out of a sense of duty; b) Both answers are possible – again, could be guilt rather than real liking; c) For; d) Against; e) Against ; f) Both answers are possible; g) Both answers are possible – he speaks for Lennie to protect him; h) For

LENNIE [p. 23]

1.

Quality	Moment/s in story	Quotation
a) Child-like	Making patterns in the water which amuse him	'Look, George. Look what I done.' (p. 3)
b) Frightened	Fighting Curley	'Lennie gave a cry of terror.' (p. 69)
c) Powerful	When he kills the puppy	'I didn't bounce you hard.' (p. 92)
d) Cunning	When he tells George he can go off and live in a cave somewhere so as to make George tell him he doesn't have to	'If you don't want me, you only jus' got to say so …' (p. 14)
e) Angry	When Crooks tells Lennie George might get hurt	'Lennie stood over him. "What you supposin' for? Ain't nobody goin' to suppose no hurt to George."' (p. 79)

3.

'seemed bewildered': Lennie is **innocent** about the world and struggles to make connections between his **clumsy** actions and their effects.

'whispered in fright': Lennie is very **anxious** about the implications of his actions.

CANDY [p. 24]

1.

a) T; b) F; c) T; d) NEE; e) T; f) NEE; g) T

2.

a) We can make a comparison between Candy and his dog because **both are old, and no longer fit for doing the jobs they could once do.**

b) We can tell Candy is upset when the dog is shot from the way he **turns away and looks at the wall, and won't sit with the other men.**

c) Candy's offer of his money for the farm is important because **it means the dream can be a reality as they will be able to contact the owner and put a deposit down.**

d) When Curley's wife comes into Crooks's room, Candy stands up to her which shows **he suddenly feels a sense of pride and optimism about the future, and sees that Crooks shouldn't be treated badly.**

ANSWERS

CURLEY [p. 25]

1.

a) Curley's wife; b) Whit; c) Carlson; d) Lennie; e) George

2.

a)

- Both views can be argued but Curley seems deeply unpleasant and possessive, so he drives his wife into chatting with Lennie as she's lonely.
- Lennie is the one who actually kills her, so he can't be absolved of blame.

b)

- He makes no attempt to touch her or show any sympathy towards her directly.
- His first instinct is to kill Lennie in as violent a way as he can.

CURLEY'S WIFE [p. 26]

1. and 2.

flirtatious p. 34; beautiful p. 35; cruel pp. 88–9; lonely pp. 85, 94; innocent (in the sense of naive) p. 96; innocent (in the sense of simple and untainted) p. 101

3.

Curley's wife is never given a **name** *which adds to the feeling that we only see her through men's eyes. She first appears when she comes into the* **bunk house** *pretending to look for Curley. George warns Lennie to keep away from her, and calls her 'jail bait' which suggests she could lead him into* **trouble**. *Later, George says the* **ranch** *isn't a suitable place for a young woman with so many men around. If we judge solely by what the men say, it is clear they think she is always* **flirting** *with them when Curley isn't around. However, when she talks with* **Lennie** *in the barn, a different side of her comes out; here she seems more vulnerable and seems to want companionship.*

CROOKS [p. 27]

1.

a) horse; b) black; c) dictionary, civil code; d) distance; e) heaven

MINOR CHARACTERS [p. 27]

1.

a) Carlson; b) the boss; c) Whit

PART FOUR: KEY CONTEXTS AND THEMES [pp. 29–31]

KEY CONTEXTS [p. 29]

1.

b)

2.

a)

3.

a)

- It meant many people lost their savings and homes.
- It forced a lot of people onto the road looking for work, e.g. George and Lennie.

b)

- It could refer to the specific plans of Lennie and George, or Curley's wife's hopes of being a film star.
- By referring to 'mice' and 'men' it reminds us of the dead mouse

that Lennie 'pets' and how human life is as fragile as the mouse.

c)

- It creates a theatrical and intimate setting where the reader can focus on the characters and their relationships.
- It allows Steinbeck to explore the workings of ranch life in this difficult economic period.

KEY THEMES [pp. 30–1]

1.

Likely choices: human fragility, dreams and reality, racial prejudice, loneliness, friendship, hope, despair

3.

Possible additions:

'little piece of lan'' – hope – people's needs are small, but this represents hope and freedom

'nobody gets no land' – the universal condition – people don't get what they want

'It's just in their head.' – dreams and reality – dreams dominate reality, as is shown by the events of the book

4.

a) *George catching Lennie with a dead mouse at the start of the novel*

Links to: fragility of life

Why: small creatures are easily killed, as is Curley's wife – almost as if she were a pet or helpless animal herself.

b) *The shooting of Candy's dog*

Links to: fragility of life

Why: The dog is shot when it has no more use; similarly, the puppy offered to Candy comes from a litter in which most of the puppies have been drowned.

Links to: loneliness

Why: Candy's dog was the only real friend and companion he had.

c) *The game of cards in the bunk house*

Links to: fragility of life; loneliness/companionship

Why: despite being 'tough', the men play cards to avoid dealing with the shooting of the dog; they play to keep each other company, as they do the 'horseshoe' game.

d) *Whit seeing that one of the ex-ranch hands has a letter in the magazine*

Links to: dreams/reality; pessimism/optimism

Why: the ranch hands like to imagine there is a 'better world' out there which they can escape to, as represented by a former ranch hand; Whit shows his excitement, but the reality is, it is just a very basic letter.

PART FIVE: LANGUAGE AND STRUCTURE [pp. 33–6]

LANGUAGE [pp. 33–5]

1.

symbol = Candy's old dog represents companionship

imagery = 'Lennie dabbled his big paw in the water'

irony = '... a manure pile under the window. Sure, it's swell.'

colloquial = 'An' you ain't gonna do no bad things like you done in Weed, neither.'

theme = 'Dreams and reality'

paradox = Lennie kills Curley's wife, but could be said to be 'innocent'

2.

a) M; b) S; c) M; d) N; e) S

4.

a) In order – 2, 1, 3

It is also well chosen because it uses an image from the natural world which is appropriate for the rural setting.

b) In order – 3, 1, 2

It is also well chosen because 'tight' has a range of connotations as in fixed and secure but also tense and under pressure, which implies the burden George is carrying.

5.

a) sight; b) touch; c) sound; d) touch; e) taste; f) sound; g) texture, smell

STRUCTURE [p. 36]

1.

a) VS; b) NS; c) VS; d) VS; e) VS; f) S

2.

b) 1; a) 2; c) 3; f) 4; e) 5; d) 6

PART SIX: GRADE BOOSTER [pp. 38–45]

WRITING SKILLS [pp. 38–9]

2.

Student A: mid

- Clear point and provides evidence in the form of a quotation
- Explanation isn't developed or explained in more detail

Student B: higher

- Clear point with appropriate quotation for evidence
- Specific comment on particular words from quote, a 'verb' and 'adverb' and explanation of effect

4., 5., 6.

Steinbeck **suggests** *that Lennie lacks understanding of the world when he says to Crooks, 'Why ain't you wanted?' This* **implies** *that he doesn't* **recognise** *prejudice. It also* **demonstrates** *that he doesn't understand himself or he would* **comprehend** *that he is different too. This* **tells us** *that Crooks and he are linked, even if they don't see it.*

SPELLING, PUNCTUATION AND GRAMMAR [pp. 40–1]

3.

We see how Lenny is magnetised by **Curley's** *wife when she comes into Crooks's room as it says he 'watched her, fascinated …'. The* **development** *of this idea is an omen of the* **tragedy** *to come as it once again* **highlights** *her central* **role** *in the novel, even though she's not the main* **protagonist.**

4.

When Curley's wife threatens Crooks, Steinbeck describes how he 'sat down on his bunk and drew into himself'. This implies Crooks is like a wounded animal that's seeking shelter inside his shell and doesn't want to anger, provoke or challenge its tormentor.

5. Student B

6.

Slim <u>had comforted</u> *George and* <u>told</u> *him, 'Never you mind …' after he* <u>kills</u> *Lennie. This* <u>suggested</u> *that Slim* <u>was</u> *an understanding and decent person, the only one who* <u>will recognise</u> *George's dilemma.*

Slim comforts George and tells him, 'Never you mind …' after he kills Lennie. This suggests that Slim is an understanding and decent person, the only one who recognises George's dilemma.

PLANNING AND STRUCTURE [p. 43]

3.

<u>How</u> does <u>Steinbeck present ideas</u> about <u>isolation</u> and <u>loneliness</u> in the <u>novel</u>?

4.

Suggested plan:

1) Steinbeck shows that it is seen as strange for men to travel together.

2) He describes Candy's need to keep his old dog.

3) He shows Crooks as separate from the others due to race and perhaps education.

4) He presents Curley's wife as someone isolated by gender and by her hopes/dreams.

5) The novel's ending shows companionship destroyed though it suggests Slim will offer support to George.

SAMPLE ANSWERS [pp. 44–5]

Opening paragraphs

1.

Student A – Expert viewpoint 1

Student B – Expert viewpoint 2

Writing about techniques

3.

Student A – Expert viewpoint 2

Student B – Expert viewpoint 1

07 DEC 2023 S